WITHDRAWN

WORLD ALMANAC® LIBRARY OF THE MIDDLE AGES

feudalism and Village Life

IN THE MIDDLE AGES

MERCEDES PADRINO

WORLD ALMANAC® LIBRARY

Please visit our web site at: www.worldalmanaclibrary.com
For a free color catalog describing World Almanac® Library's list of high-quality books and multimedia programs, call 1-800-848-2928 (USA) or 1-800-387-3178 (Canada). World Almanac® Library's fax: (414) 332-3567.

Library of Congress Cataloging-in-Publication Data

Padrino, Mercedes.
   Feudalism and village life in the Middle Ages / by Mercedes Padrino.
     p. cm. — (World Almanac Library of the Middle Ages)
   Includes bibliographical references and index.
   ISBN 0-8368-5894-8 (lib. bdg.)
   ISBN 0-8368-5903-0 (softcover)
   1. Civilization, Medieval—Juvenile literature. 2. Feudalism—Europe—History—Juvenile literature. 3. City and town life—Europe—History—To 1500—Juvenile literature. 4. Villages—Europe—History—To 1500—Juvenile literature. I. Title. II. Series.
   CB353.A53   2005
   940'.9734—dc22
                                               2005043264

First published in 2006 by
World Almanac® Library
A Member of the WRC Media Family of Companies
330 West Olive Street, Suite 100
Milwaukee, WI 53212 USA

Copyright © 2006 by World Almanac® Library.

Produced by White-Thomson Publishing Ltd.
Editor: Walter Kossmann
Volume editor: Peg Goldstein
Designer: Malcolm Walker
Photo researcher: Amy Sparks
World Almanac® Library editorial direction: Valerie J. Weber
World Almanac® Library editor: Jenette Donovan Guntly
World Almanac® Library art direction: Tammy West
World Almanac® Library graphic design: Kami Koenig
World Almanac® Library production: Jessica Morris and Robert Kraus

Photo credits:
Akg-Image: cover and pp. 5, 8 (akg), 16 (Schuetze/Rodemann), 13, 18, 19, 20, 22, 27, 32 (British Library), 25 (Rheinisches Landesmuseum, Bonn), 29 (Heidelberg University Library), 30, 39, (Bibliothèque Nationale, Paris); Art Archive: pp. 4 (Bibliothèque Nationale, Paris/Dagli Orti), 11(Travelsite/Jarrold Publishing), 23 (Musée Condé Chantilly/Dagli Orti), 26 (British Library), 40 (University Library, Heidelberg/Dagli Orti); Bridgeman Art Library: pp. 6, 15, 41, 43, (Bibliothèque Nationale, Paris), 7 (Archivo de la Corona de Aragon, Barcelona/Index), 9 (Bibliothèque de L'Arsenal, Paris), 10 (Regensburg Museum, Regensburg/Interfoto), 12 (John Bethell), 21 (Osterreichische Nationalbibliothek, Vienna/Alinari), title page and pp. 35 (Giraudon), 36 (Louvre, Paris/Peter Willi), 37 (Palazzo Schifanoia, Ferrara/Alinari), 42 (Biblioteca Monasterio del Escorial, Madrid).

Cover: A late fifteenth-century French illustration shows peasants performing various rural tasks, such as plowing and turning the soil, reaping, sheep shearing, and harvesting apples.
Title page: Peasants eat a meal in the fields during the workday.

Printed in Canada

1 2 3 4 5 6 7 8 9 09 08 07 06 05

Contents

Words that appear in the glossary are printed in **boldface** type the first time they occur in the text.

Source References on page 45 give bibliographic information on quoted material. See numbers ([1]) at the bottom of quotations for their source numbers.

he Middle Ages are the period between ancient and early modern times—the years from about A.D. 500 to 1500. In that time, Europe changed dramatically. The Middle Ages began with the collapse of the **Roman Empire** and with "**barbarian**" tribes invading from the north and east. In the early years of the Middle Ages, western European farmers struggled to survive. This period ended with European merchants eagerly seeking new international markets, European travelers looking for fresh lands and continents unknown to them to explore, European artists creating revolutionary new styles, and European thinkers putting forward powerful new ideas in religion, government, and philosophy.

What Were the "Middle Ages" Like?

Some people view the period as the "Dark Ages," an era marked by ignorance and brutality. It is true that **medieval** people faced difficult lives marred by hard work, deadly diseases, and dreadful wars, but their lives included more than that.

The Middle Ages were also a time of growing population, developing technology, increasing trade, and fresh ideas. New villages and towns were built; new fields were cleared; and, with the help of new tools like the wheeled iron plow, farms produced more food. **Caravans** brought silks and spices from faraway lands in Asia. New sports and games, such as soccer,

golf, chess, and playing cards, became popular. Musicians, singers, acrobats, and dancers entertained crowds at fairs and festivals. Traveling troupes performed plays that mixed humor with moral messages for anyone who would stop and listen.

Religion, education, and government all changed. Christianity spread throughout Europe and became more powerful. Another major faith—Islam—was born and carried into Europe from the Middle East. New schools and universities trained young men as scholars or for careers in the Church, medicine, and the law. Medieval rulers, judges, and ordinary citizens created **parliaments**, jury trials, and the common law. These changes in the fabric of society still shape our world today.

◀ A lord knights a young nobleman. The man on the left holds a sword—a symbol of knighthood—that the lord uses to tap the young man's shoulders, officially raising him to his new **rank**.

◀ Peasants performed many different tasks. They are seen here plowing with a team, shearing sheep, carrying newly picked apples in a bucket, turning the soil with a shovel, and mowing grass with a scythe to make hay.

Historians divide the entire period into two parts. In the early Middle Ages, from about A.D. 500 to 1000, Europe adjusted to the changes caused by the fall of the Roman Empire and the formation of new kingdoms by Germanic peoples. In these years, the Christian Church took form and Europeans withstood new invasions. In the late Middle Ages, from about 1000 to 1500, medieval life and culture matured. This period saw population growth and economic expansion, the rise of towns and universities, the building of great cathedrals and mosques, and the launching of the **Crusades**.

The Structure of Society

During the Middle Ages, Europeans saw themselves as belonging to one of three groups: those who prayed (clergy), those who fought (knights), or those who worked (peasants).

The clergy included two groups. Monks and nuns were people who dedicated themselves to praying for the salvation of humanity. Bishops and parish priests held services at local churches and comforted and advised other people.

The knightly class included kings, high nobles—such as dukes and counts—and the lower nobles who served under them. The men of this class were reared to be soldiers, and their purpose in life was to defend others. Most members of the clergy were born into the knightly class but switched groups when they joined the clergy.

Those who worked were the peasants who grew crops and tended livestock. Some were **freemen** and rented their land. Others were **serfs**. Serfs worked on a knight's land and were legally bound to stay on that land. Most merchants and artisans who lived in towns were originally free peasants and part of this class.

In medieval Europe, society was highly structured, and people were tied to each other by bonds of loyalty and duty. All people had obligations to others. Those obligations determined the kinds of relations people had with each other. Relations between knights and their lords were guided by a system historians call **feudalism** because the property a knight received from his lord was called a *feudum* in Latin. Relations between peasants and lords were governed by another system historians call **manorialism** because a **manor** included the lord's home and the nearby village and lands where peasants lived and worked.

feudalism and manorialism

 n medieval society, people of higher rank protected and ruled over those of lower rank. People of higher rank expected the lower ranks of society to pledge their loyalty to them and, in turn, protected their dependents when the situation required. People of lesser rank, on the other hand, provided money, goods, and services to their lords.

Lords and Their Knights

A knight who swore to serve another knight in exchange for land was called a **vassal**. The knight the vassal served was his lord. High nobles who owned large areas of land, such as counts or dukes, were vassals of the king. In turn, high nobles were lords of many other knights.

Nobles at all levels had certain rights and privileges. They had the right and responsibility to hear court cases and administer justice in their lands. Their courts resolved problems among their people and punished criminals. Lords issued licenses to merchants who wished to hold fairs

◄ Kings and other great nobles did not travel alone. Members of their households as well as servants traveled with them. On ceremonial occasions, they took many vassals and ladies with them. Here, Louis II of Anjou is seen with his companions about to enter Paris.

◄ The kneeling man in this picture is a knight paying homage to his new lord. During the ceremony, the lord granted a fief to his new vassal, and the vassal promised to serve his lord.

and markets in their lands. They kept the legal and license fees they charged. Lords also became the guardians of widows and children of vassals who died, and they kept the profits from their vassals' manors until the children became adults.

Lords had certain duties to their vassals. They were expected to give vassals a *feudum*, or **fief**. Typically, fiefs were the right to use and govern lands and manors, but some knights received a position in the lord's household or even yearly cash payments instead. Lords were expected to defend vassals who were charged with misdeeds in another lord's court or a Church court. Nobles also had to make sure that their knights were properly trained and armed for battle. If a vassal were captured by the enemy, the lord was expected to pay part of his ransom.

When a knight became a vassal, he went through a special ceremony, paying **homage** to, or honoring, his new lord. The new vassal took an oath of **fealty**, or loyalty, and was expected to follow a special code of behavior. He promised not to hurt his lord in any way, such as by revealing secrets about his lord's castles or preventing his lord from handing out justice within his realm.

A vassal was also expected to provide aid and counsel whenever his lord needed him. For instance, vassals were expected to fight when the lord went to war. They often had to perform **garrison** duty in the lord's castle for two or three months of the year or escort the lord or his family when they traveled. Vassals had to house the lord when he passed through their lands. They typically provided money when their lord's son was knighted, when his eldest daughter was married, and when he went on a Crusade. Vassals paid the lord a fee when they inherited the lands their families controlled. Most vassals helped try cases in the lord's court.

The Lord of the Manor and His Villagers
No matter how small their fiefs, all knights were lords of their own manors. They were expected to protect the farmers who worked their lands.

They were responsible for the maintenance and improvement of the village, such as repairing and building bridges or mills. The lord of the manor also provided his villagers with the lands they worked for themselves and the right to graze their animals on his property. At harvest time, when the peasants worked long, hard hours to gather his crops, the lord rewarded them with a feast. In one English village, 329 farmers who worked on the first day of a harvest consumed eighteen doves, a calf, a bull, a cow, seven cheeses, and almost sixty bushels of grain.

Peasants owed their lord various services and payments, although the obligations of serfs were different from those of freemen. Serfs were subject to their lords and had few legal rights. They had to accept the lord's decisions and punishments and could not sue the lord in other courts if his decisions were unfair. Serfs could not carry weapons and had to obtain the lord's approval to get married. Everything serfs had, such as animals and tools, technically belonged to the lord. Serfs

▼ This book illustration from around 1450 shows peasants talking with the lord of the manor about cutting grain. The peasants are holding a sickle (*left*) and a scythe.

Social Status among Peasants

Freedom was a source of status within a village but not the only source. Serfs and freemen often married one another, so it was sometimes difficult to know whether a person was free or a serf after two or three generations. The amount of property a person controlled was a second source of status. Serfs and freemen sold each other parts of the land they got from the lord, as if they owned it. Lords did not interfere with the deals peasants made among themselves. By 1300, peasants who had more land or animals than others became the leading people in the village, regardless of whether they were serfs or freemen. Those without the means to support a family had the lowest status in village society.

plowed and planted the lord's lands; they gathered his crops. After the farmwork was finished, they carted surplus goods to market. They were obligated to keep their sheep in the lord's sheepfold so that all the manure would go to fertilize the lord's fields. Female serfs were sometimes required to work at the manor house, cooking or doing laundry.

Peasants in wine-producing areas tended vines, harvested grapes, and helped make grapes into wine. Peasants are seen here picking grapes. One man carries them in a basket on his back to a large tub, where another man crushes them by stepping on them. Not all manors had wine presses.

The lord collected various taxes and fees from his serfs. He received a fee when his serfs got married, when they died, and when a son took possession of the land his parents had worked. The most hated of all taxes was the **tallage**. The lord could impose it on his serfs whenever he wished and charge as much as he wished without giving a reason. Peasants paid fees for using the lord's property, which they were forced to use. For instance, they had to grind their grain in the lord's mill and press their grapes in his wine press. They also paid a fee whenever they brought a legal matter before the manorial court. Payments were made in cash or goods, such as cheese, eggs, ale, bread, or woolen cloth.

Free tenants were peasants who rented land from the lord, but they were not subject to his will. They paid their rent with money or labor,

THIRTEENTH-CENTURY SERMON

"You lords, you deal sometimes so ill with your poor folk, and can never tax them too high; you would wish to tax them higher and higher. It is far better that you should take small taxes every year; and collect these all the more carefully. You cannot till the land yourselves, therefore you should so deal with your folk that they serve you gladly."
Friar Berthold von Regensburg [3]

especially at harvest time. Freemen, unlike serfs, had the right to carry arms and were expected to serve as foot soldiers in times of war. Like knights, freemen had the right to appeal their lord's legal decisions in higher courts.

the lord's manor

Most medieval people lived in the country on a manor. It was the place where they grew up, worked, and relaxed. The manor house was the lord's home and his place of business. From there, he managed his lands and ruled his people.

A Home and a Business

Peasants rarely traveled far from their manor and local market town. The manor was both their home and their workplace. Knights who had only one manor ordinarily made it their home, too, but many lords had various manors scattered over large areas. They usually made one manor their principal residence but lived in other manors for part of the year.

Manors not only produced food for the humans and animals who lived there but also made many specialized items that lords could sell for a profit. Surplus food was sold in local towns. In some areas, manors supplied wool for the international cloth industry. In other areas, crops were grown for cash. In France, for example, grapes for wine were planted extensively in the Burgundy and

the Wool Industry

The medieval wool industry employed shepherds, merchants, and weavers. Merchants from Flanders (in today's Belgium, France, and the Netherlands) purchased English wool. The wool was woven into cloth that was then sold in markets across Europe. In the thirteenth century, England also became an important producer and seller of woolen cloth. Perhaps the most successful wool merchants lived in Florence, Italy. They bought both English and Spanish wool and manufactured high-quality, expensive cloth. They sold their cloth in Europe, Asia, and Africa. in Europe but also in Asia and Africa.

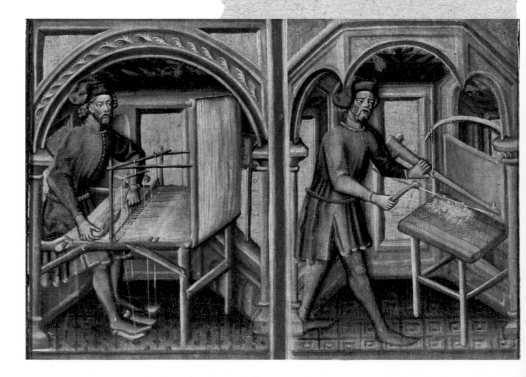

▶ This painting shows two fifteenth-century craftsmen in the woolen industry working outside a church. The man on the left is weaving, and the one on the right is spinning with a spindle.

◄ This English manor house was built in 1330. Its defenses included walls of stone and timber and a **moat**. The brick chimneys with several different flues were added in a later century.

Bordeaux regions, while herbs to make dyes were cultivated around Toulouse. The region around the Baltic Sea produced salted fish for sale in other parts of Europe.

Not all manors were the same. Manors differed in size and resources. The basic manor had its own village and a combination of the following features: the lord's manor house, a church, a gristmill, a bake oven, a wine or olive press, fields for growing crops, pastureland, a stream or other source of water, forestland, marshes, meadows, and rough **waste**. Some manors were owned by abbeys (monasteries), and their lords were abbots, the heads of abbeys. Nor were men the heads of all manors—**abbesses**, heiresses, and widows could control their own lands.

The Manor House

From the eleventh to the fourteenth centuries, manor houses were built for defensive purposes. The amount of fortification depended on how secure the region was. In some areas, houses and outbuildings were surrounded by a simple wall and ditch. Other manors had **parapets**, moats, and gatehouses. By the fifteenth century, manor houses were generally built without fortifications, although some had fences or moats to keep livestock from wandering off or deer from raiding the gardens.

The lord's house was set apart from the villagers' homes and was large and solid, having been built of timber or stone. The hall was the most important room. There, the lord's court met, meals were served, and guests were entertained. Near the hall were the buttery and larder, which were used to store food, drink, table utensils, and linens. The house had one or more bedrooms and privies (toilets), depending on the wealth of the lord and the size of his household. The family chapel was sometimes part of the house and sometimes next to it.

The courtyard around the house held the kitchen and bake house. Other outbuildings usually included a dairy, where butter and cheese were made; granaries for storing grains and hay; a stable for housing animals, wagons, and equipment; a sheepfold; a poultry house for chickens and geese; and a dovecote for housing pigeons. The lord's orchard and vegetable garden were also nearby.

The typical manor house had very few pieces of furniture. In the hall, **trestle tables** and benches were set up before each meal. Only the lord and possibly the lady (the lord's wife) would sit on chairs. A few more benches, stools, and chairs were scattered around the rest of the house. Chests were used for storing clothes, linens, money, and even books—as well as for sitting. Bedchambers had pegs built into the walls for hanging clothes. A few standing candlesticks provided light.

The most important item of furniture was usually the lord and lady's bed with its linen hangings. Beds were often taken apart and put together again when the lord and lady traveled from manor to manor. The feather mattress,

Introduction of the fireplace

Before the twelfth century, European buildings did not have fireplaces. A hearth, or fire pit, was built on the ground in the middle of a room and surrounded by stones, tiles, or bricks. The smoke went out through a small opening in the roof, and the hearth was covered at night to prevent fires. Advances in construction during the twelfth century allowed the hearth to be moved against a fireproof masonry (stone or brick) wall. A hood and chimney collected the smoke and carried it outside. The kitchens of manor houses had very large fireplaces, often big enough to roast an entire deer or ox.

▼ The hall of a manor house had to be large enough to fit the lord's household and guests at meals and to accommodate vassals and other people who came for court. The furniture was set up according to the purpose for which the hall would be used.

◄ This illustration shows a lord giving instructions to one of his manor officials as peasants pick apples. Lords wanted bailiffs and other manor officers to supervise the serfs carefully and not allow mishaps, such as pigs getting into the newly harvested crop.

pillows, sheets, and covers were also of great value. The bedding provided for others in the household depended on the person's rank. The lady's maids slept in trundle beds in the lord and lady's chamber or in their own bedroom. People slept on feather bedding, straw pallets, or just bundles of straw on the ground.

Administration of the Manor

Wealthier lords delegated the management of their manors to **estate stewards**. Estate stewards of lay (nonreligious) nobles were usually knights; those of religious lords were monks or priests. Stewards were educated men who represented their lords in legal matters and supervised all the manors that made up the lord's **estate**. They visited each manor several times a year to monitor its activities. They also presided over the manorial court.

The person responsible for running the manor was the bailiff. He was generally appointed on the recommendation of the steward and was typically the younger son of a knight or the son of wealthy peasants. Bailiffs had to read and write in order to keep the accounts of the manor. They were charged with protecting the manor and its people from attack and with collecting the rents and fees owed by the peasants. Their primary concern was the lord's **demesne**—the **arable** land reserved and cultivated for the lord. Bailiffs lived in the manor house and entertained the lord's guests in his absence.

Several village officers assisted the bailiff. These were serfs who were elected by their neighbors. The most important officer was the reeve, who supervised the workers on the lord's demesne and kept its accounts. The reeve made sure that the lord's animals and farm tools were well cared for. Other officers helped the reeve by directing the workers or policing the fields and woods. The office of ale taster was the only one women were allowed to hold. Ale tasters checked the quality and price of the ale village women made and sold to their neighbors.

QUALIFICATIONS OF A STEWARD

"The seneschal [steward] of lands ought to be prudent and faithful and profitable, and he ought to know the law of the realm, to protect his lord's business and to instruct and give assurance to the bailiffs."
Seneschaucie, treatise on estate management, thirteenth century [4]

INSTALLMENT OF THE REEVE

"The Reeve, elected by the township to that office as the best manager and tiller, must be presented to the lord or to his Seneschal [steward], who should invest him forthwith with his office. Let him therefore not be slothful [lazy] or sleepy, but let him effectually and unceasingly strive for his lord's profit."
Fleta, treatise on law and administration, thirteenth century [5]

CHAPTER 3

Life in the Village

he kind of work that took place on a manor depended on the kind of land it had. In **woodland** country, where there was little arable land but plenty of grazing land, people raised livestock, generally sheep. In flat areas that were easy to plow and plant and harvest, people grew crops.

Woodland Villages

Woodlands, despite their name, did not always include forests. These places were often marshy lands or mountainous and rocky areas that were covered with grasses and bushes on which animals could feed. Woodland villages were often tiny—simply a cluster of houses surrounded by fields, with forests and pasture beyond.

In some parts of Europe, people raised cattle or goats. Sheepherding, however, was widespread in both England and continental Europe. Although people ate some mutton, sheep were not raised primarily for their meat. Their fleece, or wool, provided steady income, and their milk was used to make cheese and butter. When dead, the sheep fat was used for tallow to make candles, and their skins were used to make warm cloaks and bedcovers.

Open-Field Villages

Open-field country was characterized by large fields that villagers cultivated for their lords and themselves. The village itself was a cluster of small peasant homesteads built near the manor house, the church, the well, and the green, or open area. Houses were not lined up along the street. Each one was placed in any part of the homestead that left room for outbuildings and doing chores. The lord's mill was located on the stream or pond, and the bread oven and shops were situated around the village.

Surrounding the village were the open fields; typically there were three. Medieval farmers planted one field in autumn with winter grain, planted another in spring with mixed crops, and allowed the third field to lie fallow, or rest, for the year. The following year, the crops were rotated, and a different field was left fallow. This three-field system gave land time to regain its fertility. Each field was divided into sections, which were subdivided into parallel strips. All the strips within a section were planted with the same crop. Each household held strips in various parts of all three fields. This way, everyone had some good soil and some poor soil. The lord's strips were usually intermingled with the peasants' strips, although some demesnes were located in separate plots. Since one person's lands were not fenced off from another's, the fields were considered "open." Between the village and the fields were paths, hedges, ditches, and temporary fences built to prevent animals from straying onto the cultivated lands.

The mixing of strips held by different households forced the villagers to work together.

Migrant Shepherds

Many lords had great flocks of hundreds or even thousands of sheep. Lords hired migrant shepherds who guided the flocks to different pastures in winter and summer. The shepherds of the Pyrenees Mountains moved their flocks from southern France to northern Spain, far from their lords' lands. Shepherds were responsible for protecting the flocks and for negotiating the right to graze them on other people's lands. Migrant shepherds lived solitary lives, seeing only a few other shepherds with whom they shared cabins near the pastures. These men rarely married.

◀ The village of Montefioralle in Italy shows how, in mountainous areas of the Mediterranean region, buildings were clustered on hilltops so that crops could be planted in the valleys below. The fields were divided into sections that followed the contour of the land.

The community as a whole decided when and how to plow, plant, weed, and gather crops. All farmers performed the same tasks at the same time. They shared equipment and plow teams or rented them from one another. After the harvest, the villagers' animals were herded together to the fields to feed on the stubble and to manure the ground. Over time, such traditional practices were written down as village bylaws.

Beyond the fields were the common lands used by the lord and villagers. Meadows provided hay—a critical source of winter feed for livestock. Pastures provided grazing lands for summer but were often limited in open-field country. Wastes yielded not only pasture for animals but also mushrooms, greens, nuts, berries, and fruit for humans. Woods were an extremely important resource. Domestic animals, especially pigs, fed on acorns, roots, leaves, and fruit there. People consumed the wild nuts, fruit, and honey found there. The wood was used for fuel and for building tools, furniture, fences, buckets, and barrels. Tree bark was used for making rope, and tree **resin** was used for lighting lamps. The forest provided the lord with chances to hunt deer, boars, and wild fowl. Villagers hunted, too, even though it was illegal for them to do so. Village officers patrolled all of these areas to make sure no household took more than its allotted share of resources.

VILLAGE FARMING LAWS

"He who plows with oxen or any other animals beside the sown land of another, where wheat or any cereal, or leguminous crops are to be sown, must leave four furrows [strips] beside this sown land, so that, when he turns, he causes no damage. Whoever breaks this rule, shall be fined ten shillings, and will make good the damage he has done."
Montepescali, Italy, 1427 [6]

"No cattle shall come into the wheat cornfield till the corn be led away [harvested]; nor into the peas cornfield till the peas be led away, on pain of [paying for] each beast one penny to the church."
Wimeswould, England, 1425 [7]

The Village Church

People gathered for baptisms, confirmations, and burials at the Roman Catholic parish church and churchyard. Church bells marked the hours, warned villagers of danger, and called them to worship. The dead were buried in the churchyard, creating strong emotional ties between the church and the village.

The church was ordinarily a stone building. In small villages, it consisted of a single large room; in large villages, it had a nave where people gathered and a chancel where the altar was placed. Some churches had side altars on either side of the chancel. On the walls were paintings of religious stories, such as the Last Judgment. On the main altar stood an image of the patron saint of the church. There were no seats for the congregation. People brought stools, sat on the floor, or stood during services.

The village priest was given a good house to live in, with a large main hall, one or two bedrooms, a privy, and perhaps a buttery and outbuildings. Like his parishioners, the priest was a farmer and cultivated the church's strips to feed himself. He was a freeman and did not owe the lord any services or fees. The priest taught the parish children how to say prayers, and he baptized, buried, and sometimes married his parishioners. He also gave practical, everyday counseling. On Sundays, he celebrated **Mass** and other services. Rather than preaching sermons based on Bible texts, the priest often taught villagers lessons about the basic tenets of the church, such as the seven deadly sins.

◀ With its beautiful bell tower, this twelfth-century church from Catalonia, Spain, has both a nave and a chancel. The village church was often the only stone building that the villagers felt belonged to them. Village celebrations and dances were held in the church and its courtyard.

Church Taxes

Church expenses were a burden on the villagers. Peasants had to tithe—give the Church one-tenth of everything they grew or produced, such as grain, cheese, wool, geese, and pigs. At Easter, villagers paid a tax to the Church on every plow team they had. At Christmas, they provided hens. When the head of a household died, the Church took the family's second-best animal—the best went to the lord. Peasants traditionally gave gifts to the Church after confessions, weddings, and funerals. The priest was supposed to use one-third of this income to make repairs to the church building, help the poor, and pay any assistant he might have.

Village Shops

The village mill, oven, and press belonged to the lord, and the villagers were required to use them. The lord rented them to villagers who operated them and charged other villagers for their services. The miller, for example, kept a portion of the flour he ground for each customer in payment. The bailiff kept accounts of all the grain processed and carefully supervised the miller's work. The baker had the exclusive right to operate the oven. Villagers brought unbaked loaves of bread to him, and he baked them. In wine- and olive oil–producing areas, villagers were required to take their grapes and olives to the lord's press. The blacksmith also leased a forge from the lord.

Some villages had centrally located taverns where ale was sold. Most "taverns," however, were simply villagers' homes. Anyone who could obtain the necessary equipment could brew a batch of ale and put up a sign to inform the neighbors. People not only bought ale at these alehouses but also gathered there to relax and talk with neighbors at the end of the day.

Peasant Homes

Within the village, each peasant household had a homestead called a **close**. Closes varied greatly in size, according to how prosperous the families were. Closes were usually divided into two sections: one included the house, outbuildings, and an outdoor work area; the other had a vegetable garden.

The poorest peasants, or **cottars**, lived in small cottages. These were typically one- or two-room houses that measured about 10 by 20 feet (3 by 6 meters). Most villagers lived in larger houses that averaged 14 by 50 feet (4 by 15 m), but some houses measured almost 100 feet (30 m) in length. The typical house had a large central living area and two or three bays or alcoves. At one end of the house, an area was set aside for sheltering animals and storing grain or equipment. The wealthiest peasants had houses with four or five bays, a small buttery and pantry, and a barn for housing livestock. Some houses also had lofts, used for sleeping and storage, that were reached by a ladder.

Peasant houses were flimsy and had to be rebuilt regularly. Depending on available materials, they were framed in timber or had the central room built of stone. Walls were made of wattle and daub (twigs and clay) or similar materials. Lords occasionally paid for the cost of building and repairing peasants' homes.

Roofs were thatched with straw or other plant material. Thatching was cheap, but it provided an ideal spot for insects, vermin, and birds to nest. Thatch also rotted and could catch fire from

Local Markets

Although the manor produced food for its people, it was not completely self-sustaining. Both bailiff and villagers needed to purchase many items in the local market town. There they obtained iron, stone for building, salt, carts, pottery, footwear, tools, baskets, and many other raw and manufactured goods. They could also purchase animals and seed. The villagers did not need to have money but could barter their surplus produce for needed goods.

◀ Wealthy peasants are shown in this picture of a Flemish house. They have a cow stalled in a bay at the end of the house, and the people indoors are sitting in front of a fireplace. The little window in the slanted roof indicates a loft.

the smoke and ash that rose from the open hearth below.

The floors of cottages and houses were generally made of clay. Housewives spread straw on top to absorb mud and dirt as well as the droppings of pigs and chickens, which were allowed inside during the day. Peasant homes had windows without glass but with shutters, and they had sturdy wooden doors. The hearth was placed in the central living bay, although some houses had more than one hearth. Few villagers could afford a fireplace with a chimney.

Lords were responsible for providing their serfs with a minimum of furniture and farm tools and equipment. How much a serf received depended on the size of his holdings. In general, all serfs— including cottars—received a trestle table with a

tablecloth and some chests, pots, pans, and vats. Others got plows, harnesses, and even **draft animals**. Serfs bought or made the rest of the furniture and household items they needed.

Drainage Ditches

Villagers frequently built drainage ditches around their closes and between their gardens and their living areas. The ditches had other uses, however. Women washed clothes, and children played in them. Everyone used them for bathing. Although planks were placed across them so people could cross, boys sometimes crossed them by pole-vaulting instead.

◀ A blacksmith needed specialized equipment. The man on the left stands by a bellows, used to blow air on the fire, making it hot enough to soften iron. The men on the right hammer a piece of soft iron into shape. Blacksmiths made tools, ox shoes and horseshoes, and parts of carts and wheelbarrows.

Typical outbuildings were barns, sheds, and pens for animals. Grain was often stored in these buildings, and peasants did such work as milking and making butter or cheese, brewing, and even weaving in them. Outbuildings sometimes included a dower cottage for parents who had retired or a specialized building such as a smithy (blacksmith's shop) or carpenter's shop. Much of daily living took place outdoors.

The Manorial Court

The manorial court was the village council and was made up of all the tenants. The steward or bailiff presided over the court and made sure proper procedures were followed, but he had no say in the court's decisions. The court made rules for the villagers on matters not already determined by custom. Farming decisions were the most important. The court met several times each year to decide such things as when particular fields were to be planted or harvested or when livestock would be allowed to graze in the meadow. The manor court also chose the village officers. Villagers made decisions by consensus (general agreement) rather than by voting.

The manorial court handled most of the legal issues that affected the villagers. The steward's clerk kept written court records and registered different types of contracts, such as land sales or leases. Most manorial court cases involved either violations against the manor, such as plowing the

lord's land poorly, selling bad ale, or allowing cattle to trample the crops, or disagreements between villagers, such as contract or inheritance disputes.

Manorial courts also handled accusations of minor crimes like theft or assault. Major crimes—such as murder, rape, and **arson**—were tried in royal and noble courts. These "high courts" tried serfs as well as freemen and nobles. Church courts heard cases concerning marriage and moral issues.

Few peasants had contact with Church courts, however. Few peasants were formally married by a priest; most peasant couples simply agreed to be married to each other and then started housekeeping together. The Church had little authority over their marriages. In general, marriage problems and accusations of immorality among peasants were settled in the manorial court.

MANOR COURT DECISIONS

Cases of trespass—taking manor resources before the agreed time or in excessive amounts—were common complaints:

"John Shad is in mercy for [guilty of] a trespass made at Howelotesfield with his draught cattle, fine threepence."

"Rose Newman for a trespass made with her sheep in the meadow, fine threepence."

Addington Manor Rolls, England, 1433 [8]

the Lord's household

he lord and lady needed many people to help them run their affairs. Their financial advisors, the knights of their garrison, and their household staff all lived with them on the manor. As with other organizations in the Middle Ages, there were levels within the lord's household and responsibilities and duties assigned to those at each level.

Members of the Household

Noble households varied considerably. Besides the lord, the lady, and their children, other members of a noble household were knights, maidens who served as the lady's companions, and senior officials, such as the estate steward and chaplain. A large landowner also had a treasurer to help administer his finances and possibly auditors, who checked the accounts of the different manors. Clerks helped the treasurer and steward. Small landowners had smaller households, but they had the same senior officials.

In addition, lords had large domestic staffs. In small households, the lady might supervise the servants personally. Large households, however, sometimes had more than sixty servants, and

lords relied on the steward of the household to supervise all of them. Senior staff members included the chamberlain (who attended the lord in his chamber), the butler (in charge of the buttery), the marshal (responsible for the horses, stables, and outside workers), and the cook. These senior servants normally traveled with the lord, lady, and noble companions to their different manors. Other trusted members of the staff were the children's nurses, the barber, and messengers who carried letters great distances. The household also employed tailors, bakers,

▼ In this normal noble family dinner, the lord and lady sit at the table with their two chaplains, a nobleman, and two other ladies. Other members of their household would sit at other tables.

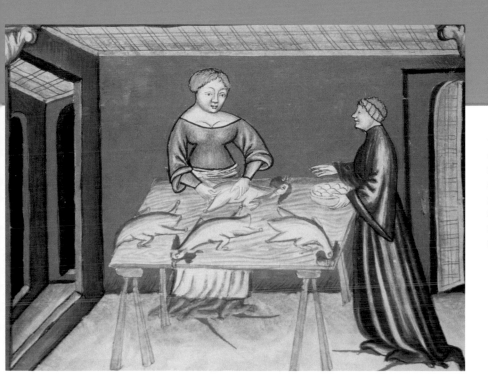

The lady supervised the cook and other servants to make sure the dishes served were abundant and reflected her family's high station. She also made sure that servants did not waste any food.

laundresses, grooms, and people who cleaned and generally helped the senior staff.

The Lord and Lady

The lord made the decisions about his lands and supervised the work of his officials. He made sure his territories were protected. He stayed in contact with his vassals, held court, and served on his overlord's court. The lord paid close attention to his rents and other income because he had many expenses. He had to pay fees to his own lord and provide **dowries** for his daughters. A lord had to leave his sons lands when he died or educate them so that they could join the clergy. One of the lord's main concerns was arranging marriages for his children with rich and powerful families that would make his own family more rich and powerful. Moreover, he was expected to maintain a high standard of living. It was a sign of status that he could feed a large household as well as guests.

When the lord was away for military reasons or other business, the lady took over management of the estate. Upon her husband's return, however, she lost her position. Although she had power and influence in the household, the lady had no legal authority.

The lady of the manor ran the household. She supervised the everyday work of the kitchen, bakery, brew house, dairy, gardens, and orchard. She made sure enough food was put aside for the winter and oversaw the purchase of cloth, spices, and other goods the manor did not produce. It was her job to see that every member of the household was properly clothed.

An important part of a noblewoman's life was entertaining guests. Guests who lived nearby sometimes came just for dinner, but many stayed for several days. Hosting guests was a way of maintaining ties with family and friends and fulfilling feudal obligations to inferiors and superiors. Entertaining guests also helped advance a family's interests. By inviting other nobles to her home, a wife could help her husband forge military alliances. If her husband had political ambitions, she could establish closer ties with influential members of his overlord's household or create opportunities for her husband to advise and help his overlord. Through her connections, the lady could find a position for a young female relative as a companion to an important noblewoman. The young woman could then learn how to act among powerful people, make influential friends,

Noble Widows

Although a noblewoman of high rank had more status than a nobleman of lesser rank, widows were the only women who could completely control their own affairs. Widows controlled their own manors and could sue others in court. A noble widow could continue to entertain, travel, and maintain her network of friends and contacts as she had when her husband was alive. Without a husband, however, she had no political influence, unless she had a son who consulted her for help and advice on political matters.

and meet a wealthy future husband. Noblewomen also fulfilled their feudal duties by exchanging letters and small gifts with other members of the nobility.

The Lord and Lady's Children

The young children of nobles had little contact with their parents. Infants were placed in the care of **wet nurses** who cared for them until age

seven or eight. The nurse took the place of the mother. Not only was she expected to feed, bathe, and attend to the child's physical needs, but also to hug, kiss, and sing the child to sleep. Wet nurses even suckled young children in place of their mothers. Children spent their early years at play. They had all sorts of toys: rattles, balls, pretty stones, dolls, and horns. Their games and entertainments included puppet shows, various ball games, hide and seek, archery, and building sand castles.

At about age seven, children began their formal education. Noble parents could send their children to boarding schools in nunneries or have their children taught at home by a tutor, perhaps the manor's chaplain, assisted by other members of the household. Sometimes mothers taught their own children. Another option was to send children to the house of relatives or friends—ideally higher in rank or more educated than the parents—for schooling. Children were not always happy with this arrangement, however. Letters from several children to their parents express their unhappiness in other people's households.

◄ In the Middle Ages, books had to be copied by hand, a very slow process. It was unlikely for a household to have more than one copy of a book. Teachers read aloud to students. Repetition and review were used so that students would remember what they were taught.

A MEDIEVAL VIEW OF CHILDREN

"[Children] keep no secrets but repeat all that they see and hear. Suddenly they laugh, suddenly they weep, and are continuously yelling, chattering, and laughing. They are scarcely silent when they are asleep. When they have been washed, they dirty themselves again. While they are being bathed or combed by their mothers, they kick and sprawl and move their feet and hands and resist with all their might. They think only about their stomachs, always wanting to eat and drink. Scarcely have they risen from bed than they desire food."
Bartholomaeus Anglicus, thirteenth-century monk [9]

William Marshal (who became one of the most admired knights of the twelfth century) cried when he was parted from his mother and siblings.

Both boys and girls learned to read, many well enough to read **romances**, poems, prayer books, and other religious books. Some children learned writing, Latin, and perhaps another local language. For example, children in England often learned French. All children learned to follow rules of etiquette and to say prayers. Boys were also given knightly training. They learned to use weapons, to care for armor, and to ride and care for horses. When they trained at another lord's house, they also learned by serving him at the table and in his chamber. Girls were taught spinning, sewing, embroidery, home medicine, and how to run a household.

Older children were still allowed to play, but parents and tutors strictly disciplined them. Children had to be completely obedient and show respect and a cheerful attitude toward their elders. There was little tolerance for sassiness, and both boys and girls were beaten if they did not behave. One English lady recalled how her parents "so sharply taunted, so cruelly threatened, yea presently sometimes with pinches, nips and bobs that I thought myself in hell."

At about age twenty-one, young men completed their training and were knighted. They then spent two or three years traveling with a group of companions chosen by their fathers to act as guides, comrades, and protectors. The group would take part in **tournaments**, local wars, and an occasional Crusade. Thus, a young knight gained practical experience as a soldier. Young women completed their education earlier. They were usually married between fourteen and sixteen years of age. By the time they were twenty, they typically had children of their own.

▶ Older children and young people were expected to practice the skills they would use as adults. Girls learned spinning, and boys learned to wrestle and fight with swords. Often their first swords were made of wood.

the peasant household

Peasant families were busy with work all year long. Everyone—even young children—helped out. Those who did not have land of their own worked for others for pay or for a portion of the harvest from the land. Even in winter, when there was no planting or harvesting, country people had other work to do.

Serfs at Home

Peasant households in open country were not very large. They tended to include a husband and wife and their children—usually no more than five people. There were exceptions and variations, however. Sometimes an elderly grandparent lived with the family, or one of the parents was widowed. Wealthier peasants might have servants or more children. The typical serf holding (property) could support only a small family, so married children and other relatives were not part of the household.

In woodland country, too, most households included only parents and children. In remote areas, such as the Pyrenees Mountains between France and Spain, though, it was common for grandparents and unmarried siblings to be part of the household as well.

Men, Women, and Work

Men's work was regulated by the seasons. The first plowing began in late winter, perhaps February. Controlling the plow and team along the strips of land required strength and skill. The plowman's wife or a son helped by prodding the animals. By May, the strips had been plowed again and planted with wheat, barley, beans, and other crops. During the week, a serf would alternate working on the lord's land and on his own. In June, he plowed the fields for winter grain. He began cutting hay in the meadow and had it stacked by early July. Summer work included weeding, another plowing of the winter fields, and **harrowing**. The harvest began in late July and lasted into early September. In October, the farmer sowed his winter wheat. November was the time for butchering pigs, followed by salting and smoking the meat. In December and January, the farmer mended tools and equipment and repaired ditches and fences. Year-round he looked after his animals.

In woodland country, too, the seasons governed work. Shepherds and herders moved their flocks to different pastures at different times of year. They planted grain, hay, and winter feed in spring and harvested them in summer and fall. In sheep-raising areas, lambs were born in December. Shepherds stayed busy caring for the ewes (female sheep) and lambs. In spring, the sheep were sheared and the fleeces stored. Around May, when the lambs were weaned (taken off their mother's milk), the shepherds began milking the ewes and making cheese.

In spite of all the time agriculture required, some men practiced other trades to make extra money for their families. Some worked as carpenters, potters, or roof thatchers. In ore-rich regions, men worked in mines. Others became **fullers** and dyers for the cloth industry. Still others sold bread or extra produce in the nearest market town.

Women also had many jobs. They worked in the fields, doing some of the same tasks as men, such as weeding and harrowing, and also some different jobs, such as binding the sheaves of grain. Around the close, women milked cows and

▶ Harvest time was a period of intense work. Men and women worked together to gather the crops. After cutting the grain, the workers tied it up in bundles and carted it back to the lord's close or to their own for **threshing** and **winnowing**.

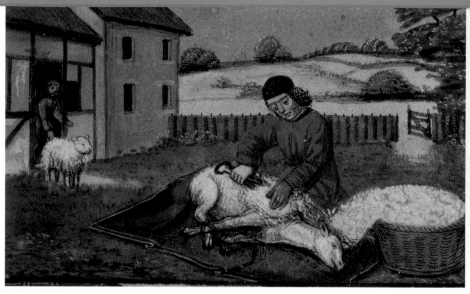

► Shearing took place after the weather began to turn warm, and the sheep did not need to grow any more wool for the summer. Ewes were highly valued because they gave both milk and wool. Male sheep were also valued because their fleeces were considered better than those of the females.

ewes and raised poultry and pigs. They planted and tended vegetable gardens. Women kept fires going and made butter and cheese. They wove cloth and sewed the family's garments. House cleaning was not time-consuming since peasants had so little furniture. Women just swept the floor and spread clean straw. For cooking and washing, they hauled heavy buckets of water home from the well, spring, or stream. Their most important job was rearing the children.

Peasant women also did work for extra income. Many women made bread and brewed ale for sale or barter. They also sold surplus eggs, cheese, and butter. The most common side activity for women was spinning thread from wool and linen, which was supplied to them by cloth manufacturers.

The Villagers' Children

Unlike the children of lords, peasant children lived with their families. Women nursed their own babies and kept them in a cradle by the fire or carried them around as they worked. The toddler years were the most difficult for parents. With tools and animals all around, it was hard to make the close safe for curious toddlers.

Between the ages of five and twelve, children spent most of their time playing. They made up games with the objects they found around them: they chased ducks and geese, jumped over ditches, and threw stones into streams. They also enjoyed archery and ball games. When they misbehaved, they were punished just as severely as the lord's children.

Starting at age four or five, boys and girls helped their mothers by feeding chickens and watching younger siblings. They began to do chores away from the close around age eight. These tasks included gathering wood, **foraging** in the waste, and helping to clean up after the harvest. Girls picked fruit in both the close and the woods. They also helped their mothers with

Fulling Mills

Fulling is the cleaning and shrinking of newly woven cloth before it is dyed and used to make clothing or linens. For centuries, fullers performed this work by rubbing fuller's earth (a fine, mineral-rich clay) on cloth and trampling it with their feet in a trough full of water. In the thirteenth century, the fulling mill was invented. In a fulling mill, a waterwheel moved hammers that beat the cloth in place of trampling it. Mills were built wherever waterpower was available, so the cloth industry spread out wherever possible into the countryside.

household tasks. Fishing, a popular amusement for boys, also brought in food. Boys herded geese, pigs, goats, and sheep and pastured and watered draft horses. Boys also began to assist the men. They prodded the plow team, weeded, and tied sheaves during the harvest. Some boys helped out the village craftspeople. Children in this age group still played, taking horseback rides or having fun in the woods and streams when they were sent off to do chores.

After age twelve, life became more serious. Teenagers continued to have time for games and amusements, but they also had to master the skills they would need as adults. Girls took increasing responsibility for grown women's jobs, such as cooking and washing clothes, allowing their mothers to spend more time on side activities that brought in extra money. Teenage boys helped their families in several ways. In woodland country, they became fully responsible for the flocks. In open-field country, they continued to fish, collect wood, and forage. As they got older and physically mature, they were

▶ This fourteenth-century illustration shows boys of different ages playing together. The younger boys wrestle, pretending to be riders mounted on the shoulders of older boys, who play the part of horses.

Academic Education

Peasant girls did not go to school. The only formal instruction they received was religious education. Occasionally, peasant boys were sent to school. Serf families had to pay a fine to the lord to send their sons to school, but the expense was worthwhile since an educated man could become a bailiff or other manor official, or even a priest.

taught to plow, use scythes, and load carts with grain. Some learned crafts from their fathers or apprenticed (trained) with another villager. By eighteen or nineteen, they worked with their fathers in the fields.

Wage Earners

Peasants who did not hold lands worked for wages. Cottars, both men and women, always needed to find a way to make ends meet. Many other villagers hired themselves out as well. Younger sons who would not inherit land had to get jobs. If his parents were still strong and did not need his help farming, the oldest son might work for pay as well, until he inherited their land. Many young women did wage work until marriage. Even prosperous peasants with animals, plows, and other equipment did paid work to earn extra money.

The manor was the principal employer. It needed regular farm workers and a domestic staff, even when the lord was not in residence. Villagers took jobs cleaning, cooking, and herding animals. Since there were never enough serfs to cultivate the entire demesne, plowmen and other farmhands were hired. Wealthy villagers also hired servants to do domestic work or to help with brewing and other side occupations. Widows and the elderly hired others to plant and harvest their strips of land. Some regular jobs were part-time, so villagers sometimes combined two. For example, a woman who milked the lord's cows and ewes part of the day might also work as a dressmaker.

CHAPTER 6

Culture and Relationships

oble or peasant, people had ideals and communities. They tried to live up to these ideals in their personal relationships. They often formed ties to others that provided comfort and pleasure.

Chivalry

Knights were supposed to have certain ideal qualities that they demonstrated by following a code of honorable behavior called chivalry. The most important of these qualities was prowess. Prowess was a combination of strength, skill with arms, and courage—all traits necessary to be a good soldier. Another important quality was loyalty. A knight was expected to fulfill his duties to his lord and his vassals. He was expected to keep his word—even to enemies. A knight was also supposed to be generous to his vassals and guests. He was supposed to provide fine meals and gifts. Courtesy toward other knights was also a key quality. The knight was to be polite and fight fairly. It was not chivalrous for two knights to fight against one or to ask a captured opponent to pay a higher ransom for his release than he could afford. Ideally, knights tried to gain glory and fame by exhibiting chivalrous qualities. In reality, they practiced chivalry in tournaments but were not likely to do so in actual battle.

The Church encouraged a religious side to chivalry. The ceremony by which a man became a knight usually took place in a church after a period of fasting and prayer. The knight's sword was blessed by a clergyman. Knights were supposed to fight for God as well as for their lord. For this reason, many of them went on Crusades. Popular poems and songs reinforced the religious side of chivalry with stories of knights who fought the Muslims in Spain or went on a quest for the Holy Grail.

Courtly Love

In the twelfth century, the philosophy of courtly love became popular among nobles. Courtly love

William Marshal

William Marshal was a knight in the service of King Henry II of England. He rose to become one of the king's closest advisers and was famous for his chivalry. When he was waiting to take his place at a tournament one day, a young official asked him for a present. Marshal then rode out and knocked his opponent off his horse. Marshal was entitled to keep the other knight's horse as his prize. Instead, he gave it to the young man who had asked him for a gift. Thus, Marshal showed both prowess and generosity.

expanded the idea of chivalry by encouraging knights to treat women with consideration and cultivate social skills. A chivalrous knight was supposed to be polite and courteous to everyone, especially ladies. The knight was supposed to sing and accompany himself on a musical instrument. He had to be able to flirt and talk about love. In addition, he was supposed to

ADVICE TO A COURTLY LOVER

"In ladies' service labor and take pains;
Honor and champion them; and if you hear
Calumnious [damaging] or spiteful talk of them
Reprove the speaker; bid him hold his tongue.
Do what you can damsels and dames to please.
Let them hear you narrate most noble tales.
You'll gain a worthy reputation thus."
The Romance of the Rose [10]

perform deeds for a lady and wear a token she gave him at tournaments.

Ladies were the main promoters of courtly ideas. They sponsored **troubadours**, poets who wrote about courtly love. England's queen, Eleanor of Aquitaine, and her daughter Marie,

▲ A knight and lady talk about a poem in this portrayal of courtly love. Courtly love allowed noblemen and noblewomen to share an appreciation of poetry and music and to take part in intellectual discussions.

countess of Champagne, set the tone for other ladies. They welcomed troubadours to their households and even suggested ideas for poems to them. Their households became famous for witty and lively discussions.

Courtly romances and poems used the legends of King Arthur and the stories of ancient Greek and Roman heroes as subjects. The stories combined heroic deeds with deep love and portrayed knights and ladies unable to eat or sleep because of love. Such love was considered good because it made a knight more chivalrous and led him to perform brave deeds. In some stories, the knight wins his lady. In others—such as the story of Lancelot and Guinevere—the lovers can never be happily united.

Marriage

Legally, medieval marriages were not relationships between equals. Wives were expected to obey their husbands, and husbands were allowed to beat disobedient wives. Many tales from the period tell of shrewish wives and cruel husbands. Occasionally, wives were afraid of their husbands. Nevertheless, many couples in arranged marriages developed real affection for each other. The reality for people at all levels of society was that to run a household and prosper, husband and wife had to cooperate.

▼ This thirteenth-century illustration shows a couple being married. Weddings often took place at the church door—the most public of places—where everyone could witness them. The couple and the guests then went inside for a service.

A HUSBAND'S LAST WORDS

"More write I not unto you, but the Holy Trinity keep you now, dear and trusty wife. Here I make an end, wherefore I pray you, as my trust is wholly in you, over all other creatures, that this last will be fulfilled, and all other that I ordained at home, for all the love that ever was between man and woman."
Will of Stephen Thomas, 1417–1418 [11]

For nobles, marriages were practical matters and carefully arranged. For the high nobility, marriages were political. Payment of a dowry could mean losing control of large territories for one family and gaining control for another. A marriage could cement an important alliance. Lesser lords were also concerned with gaining and maintaining lands, wealth, and status. Sometimes the fathers of both bride and groom arranged a marriage when their children were very young. The selection of an appropriate husband for his daughter was one of the father's jobs. Another important concern was to provide a good dowry, so his daughter would not have to marry below her rank. Among noble families, the higher their rank, the larger the dowry they expected to receive from their brides.

Widows who wished to remarry generally had more freedom to choose their husbands than they

ADVICE TO HUSBANDS AND WIVES

"And she must go to market, to sell . . . [the surplus products] And also to buy things needed by the household, and to give her husband a true account of what she has spent. And if the husband should go to market to buy or sell, than he, too, must account to his wife in the same way. For if they deceive each other, they deceive themselves, and are unlikely to prosper."
Anthony Fitzherbert, Boke of Husbandrie, c. 1500 [12]

had had with a first marriage. Men who were financially independent could choose their own wives. They often chose brides who were much younger than they were.

Peasants were freer than nobles to marry for love. The wealth and status of the spouse's family were taken into account, but the spouse's character was just as important. Young men and women courted and got to know each other, then asked for their parents' blessing. Before they could marry, men had to acquire enough land to support a family, which usually happened when their fathers died or retired. Thus men usually married later than women. The bride's father usually gave a dowry of money or household or farm goods. Sometimes single women saved their wages for several years until they had enough money for their dowries.

Peasant Guilds

Peasant guilds were social and religious associations. They brought together people with a common interest. Some guilds were for people in the same occupation, such as field workers or miners. Young men or young women sometimes formed their own social groups. In some villages, any adult who paid dues could be a member of the village guild. Guild members felt responsible for each other and called one another brother and sister. Guilds imposed rules of moral and polite behavior on members. Parties in a dispute were supposed to consult the head of the guild for help in solving the problem.

Guilds provided significant benefits. Members visited sick brothers and sisters, and guilds covered the costs of members' funerals—a major expense for most families. With the dues it collected, a guild purchased and maintained a herd of cattle. It then lent its members oxen for plowing—an important benefit since most people could not afford a whole team themselves. Guilds also gave business loans in the form of money or products, such as grain or malt, which members could use to make bread or ale for sale.

food and drink

or people at all levels of society, bread was the basis of every meal. It was even the plate! Instead of dishes, diners ate off thick slices of old bread, called trenchers. The trenchers softened as they absorbed the juices and sauces from the food.

Dinner with a Knight

The lord's household ate large quantities of bread at every meal. The bread served to nobles, however, was much finer than the bread given to servants. Meat was the second most important part of meals. The knightly class ate beef and mutton often and pork, veal, and poultry less frequently. Game, such as venison and partridge, was a special treat rather than a staple. Often the meat was salted. Joints of meat or birds were roasted whole on a spit or were cut up and cooked with liquid in a pot. They were also baked in pies.

People ate fish as well. Inland people ate freshwater fish from ponds or streams, but they also ate ocean fish that had been salted, smoked, or dried. People who lived near the coast had a far greater variety of fresh fish and shellfish. Other important sources of protein were cheese and eggs.

Vegetables and fruits were not always plentiful. Garden greens and most fruit had to be eaten in season, so choices were limited in winter. Roots—like turnips, carrots, and onions—

▼ Visits from high nobles were occasions for feasting. Here, King John I of Portugal entertains the Duke of Lancaster. The rectangle on the table in front of each diner is his trencher. The round buns—made from lighter flour—were the bread they actually ate.

Preserving with Salt

After a large animal was slaughtered, the meat was treated with salt to keep it from spoiling. In one process, the salt was pounded very fine by hand. Then the meat was coated with it and left to rest in a tub of salt. A second way of preserving meat was to place it in a strong brine—a mixture of salt and water. No matter which method was used, the meat had to be soaked and rinsed well to get the excess salt off before cooking.

stayed fresh in the cold. Peas and beans could be dried and later cooked into thick soups with bacon, vegetables, and spices.

People everywhere drank alcoholic beverages. In wine-producing areas, the entire household drank wine. In areas that did not produce wine, knights and ladies drank imported wine, and the domestic staff drank ale or beer. Nobles drank ale as a thirst quencher any time of day. Milk was reserved for children and cooking. Some people drank cider or mead, an alcoholic drink made from honey.

A MEDIEVAL KNIGHT'S DINNER

"Then attendants set a table upon trestles broad,
And lustrous white linen they laid thereupon,
A saltcellar of silver, spoons of the same.
He washed himself well and went to his place,
Men set his fare before him in fashion most fit.
There were soups of all sorts, seasoned with skill,
Double-sized servings, and sundry fish,
Some baked, some breaded, some broiled on
*   the coals,*
Some simmered, some in stews, steaming
*   with spice,*
And with sauces to sup that suited his taste."
Sir Gawain and the Green Knight,
fourteenth century [13]

Medieval people liked spicy food. They grew sage, borage, mustard, and many other herbs in their gardens. Wealthy people purchased a tremendous variety of spices from Asia, including pepper, cinnamon, and cumin, and other spices with exotic names, such as zedoary (a bitter plant) and grains of paradise (a peppery seed). Herbs and spices were used in combination. People also flavored wine and other drinks with them and used them to make medicines. Cooks used honey and sugar in both main dishes and desserts.

Asian spices were luxury items and very costly. Some foods grown in Europe became luxuries when shipped to other areas. For example, almonds, rice, and figs, which grew in Spain and Italy, were very expensive in northern Europe. Due to their value, these items were locked away. Every day, the cook had to ask for the luxury items needed for that day's meals and account for their use to the household steward every night. Serving luxury items emphasized the lord's status and wealth.

Mealtime at the Manor House

In a manor house, the day began with morning Mass. Afterward, members of the household picked up some bread and wine or ale for breakfast. They ate individually; a formal meal was not served. Children and the sick were the only ones served a bigger breakfast by servants. The main meal of the day, dinner, was served in the late morning. The entire household gathered in the hall to eat it. The lord, lady, guests, and principal members of the household sat at the head table. Other people sat at tables according to their rank.

The tables were set with cloths, spoons, cups, and dishes of salt. People at the head table used utensils made of silver; those at the other tables used wooden utensils. Servants brought the food out in two or three courses, and each course included several dishes. No one was expected

lighting the hall

Not many candles were used in the evening during supper. In the households of high nobles, only a single large candle was placed on the head table. The rest of the room was lighted with rush lights and cresset lamps. Rush lights were made from the stems of grasses covered with animal fat. Cresset lamps were made of metal. They were filled with oil and had multiple wicks.

to eat everything, but by offering people plenty of choices and large amounts of food, a lord demonstrated how generous he was. The food was served onto plates that were shared by two people, who then ate individual portions from their trenchers. After the meal, servants gave the leftovers and trenchers to the poor.

Supper was eaten in the early evening, before it got very dark. Supper was not as formal as dinner, and just a few dishes were served. It was an important social time, however, when friends talked and relaxed together.

Medieval people were finicky about table manners. People ate most foods with their hands, so all were given towels and expected to wash their hands before and after eating. Certain foods had to be eaten with specific fingers to leave other fingers clean for different dishes. Drinking cups were shared, so it was essential to wipe one's mouth well before drinking and to hold a cup properly when handing it to another person. Service was very precise, too. The lord's squire (personal attendant) served him and the lady. Other pairs of diners followed special rules: a person of lower rank served one of higher rank, and a man served a woman. Everyone had to be cheerful and polite.

The Peasant Table

Even more than lords, peasants filled up on bread. Their bread was coarse, usually made from a mix of grains. It was sometimes made from peas and beans. These same products were used

to make porridge. Poor cottars often ate porridge (made from boiling grains) to avoid having to pay the miller to grind their grain.

Unlike nobles, villagers did not eat meat very often. The meat from a pig or ox that was salted or smoked in the fall had to last for a number of months. Chickens and geese were needed for their eggs. Cheese and eggs were important sources of protein for many peasants. They supplemented these foods with fish, doves, and game they poached (hunted illegally) in the lord's woods.

Villagers ate the same home-grown fruits and vegetables as their lords did—cherries, plums, and pears in the north; quinces, oranges, and lemons along the Mediterranean Sea. Peasants ate many vegetables in season. Almost anything—even strawberry leaves—went into their pots. They ate peas and beans fresh after the harvest and then ate them dried in the winter. Women preserved cabbage by pickling it in brine and making sauerkraut.

For seasoning food, peasants used salt, honey, vinegar, and herbs. For very special occasions, a farm wife might buy some spices. A peasant's daily drink was usually ale, wine, or cider that was made locally. Both adults and children sometimes drank milk.

Villagers normally ate three times each day. They probably ate breakfast at dawn before starting work. This meal consisted of bread, cheese, and an onion or other vegetable, plus a drink. Dinner, their heaviest meal, was at noon. It usually consisted of bread and a thick soup made from greens, turnips, beans, onions, and perhaps a piece of meat or bone. The evening's supper was usually made up of leftovers from dinner as well as more bread and cheese.

Fasting and Feasting

The Church calendar called for many days of fasting. For example, during Lent (the forty days before Easter), Advent (the twenty-four days before Christmas), and every Friday, Christians were supposed to fast. In practice, fasting meant that people did not eat meat. In manors, a variety

▲ During harvest time, when both men and women were gathering the crop, peasants did not have time to cook or go home to eat a large meal. They ate bread and cheese in the fields. The lord provided their main meal at the end of the workday.

of seafood dishes were served instead of meat. Fewer courses were also served. In some ways, fasting affected the lord's household more than the villagers, who ate little meat to begin with.

The Church calendar also had days of feasting, and people celebrated weddings and other events. Banquets given by nobles followed complicated ceremonies. Trumpets and drums announced each new course. Musicians and performers put on elaborate shows. Banquets lasted hours and could include many courses with ten to twenty dishes each.

Expensive and unusual foods were served at banquets along with more familiar meats. Seafood sometimes included whale, porpoise, and seal. Wild birds of all sorts were served, among them crane, heron, eagle, and swan. Banquets also provided surprises. Live birds were put inside baked pie shells—to fly out when the pies were cut. Mythological animals were created by sewing parts of different roasted animals together. Sometimes sculptures made from pastry, sugar, or papier-mâché were paraded about the hall.

Village feasts were not as elaborate, but peasants also celebrated holidays ("holy days"). A community gathered at a village feast would likely enjoy a great variety of food in large quantities. Beef, veal, mutton, lamb, pork, rabbit, and eggs might all be served. Butter, cream, and honey were used in the preparation. The sponsors might even splurge on imported items, such as dates, pepper, and cloves. Feasts gave villagers a chance to enjoy many special treats.

A LAMENT FOR LENT

"Thou wilt not believe how weary I am of fish, and how much I desire that flesh were come in again, for I have ate none other but salt fish this Lent, and it has engendered so much phlegm within me that it stops my pipes [so] that I can neither speak nor breathe."
English schoolboy, fifteenth century [14]

35

CHAPTER 8

What People Wore

 ords and peasants alike used clothes as a way of displaying their wealth and importance. Clothes were generally made of wool or linen, but a variety of fabrics were made from both materials, ranging in quality. Fine fabrics, colored with expensive dyes, were a visible sign of high status.

Noble Fashions

Clothing was a major expense for both knights and ladies. In their wills, people commonly left articles of clothing to their favorite relatives. There was no shame in wearing such hand-me-downs.

Men and women wore very similar clothing. Basically, they dressed in layers. Over their underwear, they wore tunics (full-length robes) with long narrow sleeves. A second tunic went over the first. It had wide sleeves or was sleeveless like a jumper. For winter, the second tunic was trimmed or lined with fur. Narrow belts called girdles were worn over the tunics. They rested on the hips, and people hung pockets and keys from them. A mantle, or cape, was next, also trimmed or lined with fur. It was fastened at the neck with a chain or brooch. Stockings and slippers were worn in the house. Outdoors, people wore boots. Both men and women wore linen head coverings indoors. They put on heavier hoods and caps to go outside. People of both sexes wore gloves, fur lined if possible. Everyone favored bright colors.

There were a few differences between men's and women's clothing. Men wore linen drawers, close-fitting underpants held up by a belt or drawstring. On their heads, they wore a coif, a cap tied under the chin, both indoors and outdoors. The coif was very practical for knights because it kept their long hair neat.

> ### a lady's toilette
> Medieval noblewomen used a variety of beauty supplies. Their basic cosmetics were skin whiteners and rouge. They used rosewater and sheep fat to protect their skin. Some women used hair-removing pastes, while others used razors to remove unwanted body hair. In their beauty kits, women also kept combs, tweezers, mirrors, and cotton for applying skin products.

▶ Jewelry, like this gold and enamel dragon medallion, was commonly given as a gift to both men and women. It was a sign of rank to wear it and to be able to afford to give it to others.

▲ This picture shows how medieval fashions were changing by 1470. Wimples and hoods were replaced by more fanciful hats and headdresses. Garments lost their simple lines. Men and women, however, did not lose their love of bright colors.

Women wore linen chemises—loose, full-length slips—under their clothes. On their heads, they wore veils or wimples—head wraps that covered the hair, neck, and chin.

Men and women both wore jewelry, which was an important way of displaying one's wealth and rank. Pins, gold rings, and necklaces were popular. Brooches, used to fasten clothes, were often elaborate jewels. Girdles were also a type of jewelry. They were made of expensive fabrics and had a lot of embroidery, perhaps with gold or silver thread. Some girdles were made of gold and precious stones.

Most knights and ladies wore clothes made of fine wool. Silk was so expensive that usually only kings and the wealthiest nobles could afford entire outfits made of it. The type of fur on a garment was also a sign of rank and wealth. Only kings could wear ermine. Lords generally wore squirrel, and ladies wore miniver (a white fur) or other furs. Fur was not just a luxury. It was worn indoors because houses were not heated. For men, the length of clothing was another sign of status. On formal occasions, kings wore robes that reached the floor. Ordinarily, high nobles showed their ankles, and other knights wore their tunics to about mid-calf. Women's clothes were always long.

Over time, fashions changed. Belts with metal buckles replaced girdles. Men's tunics became shorter. By the fifteenth century, they looked more like fitted jackets with skirts. Hats and turbans replaced hoods and caps. Trains and huge sleeves were added to women's over-tunics. Waistlines were raised. Women started wearing tall pointed caps with veils and headdresses shaped like horns or hearts. Starting with the thirteenth century, people began to use buttons to secure clothes and as decorations.

Peasant Garments

Villagers wore sturdy, durable clothing for work. Their underclothes were made of linen, and their outer garments of coarse wool. Men wore breeches—long, loose pants that could be pulled up to the knees. They wore knee-length tunics, with perhaps a shorter, snugger over-tunic on top. They wore belts, hoods, and straw hats. Women wore long gowns with belts. Sometimes they wore sleeveless tunics over their gowns. On their heads, they wore wimples. Both men and women wore stockings and shoes or boots with wooden soles. In winter, they wore sheepskin cloaks and woolen hats and mittens.

The clothing peasant families owned varied considerably. The poorest peasants did not always have warm clothing for winter. Servants at a manor house received clothes as part of their salaries as well as some of their lord's and lady's hand-me-downs. Prosperous peasants

Sumptuary Laws

Sumptuary laws dictated the types of clothing and foods that people at all levels of society could have—from nobles to serfs. The laws were very detailed. For example, they stated the quality of the fabric and how much embroidery a knight's tunic could have. The laws did not work, however. From lesser nobles to peasants, people ignored them and acquired the best clothing, food, and household furnishings they could afford.

bought good-quality wool and even some silk for their garments. They frequently owned some jewelry. Besides their work clothes, serfs typically had a few nice articles in bright colors for holidays and special occasions.

Cleaning Clothes

Doing laundry was hard work. Linen underwear and head coverings were soaked, boiled, beaten, and rubbed clean. Women made soap from animal or vegetable fat and lye, a chemical made from wood ashes and water. They brushed and sheared woolen clothes to get the dirt off. They used hot stones as irons.

A WRITER'S DESCRIPTION OF A POOR PLOWMAN

"I saw a poor man hanging on to the [plow]. His coat was of coarse stuff called cary. His hood was full of holes, and his hair stuck out of it. As he trod the soil, his toes stuck out of his worn shoes with their thick soles; his hose hung about his hocks [shins]. . . . He had two mittens made of rough stuff, with worn-out fingers thick with muck."
William Langland, *Piers the Ploughman*, fourteenth century [15]

▶ Peasants' everyday clothing did not change much over the centuries. Made by busy housewives, it was simply cut and loose enough to give freedom of movement.

CHAPTER 9

Entertainment

eople of all classes enjoyed parties, music, and games. Adults often played the same games as children. Activities like swimming and archery were not only fun but also were useful life skills.

Poetry and Music

The poems the troubadours wrote were set to music. Typically, a single musician sang the melody. Some songs had a refrain, or chorus, and other singers joined in. As troubadours spread ideas about courtly love from southern France to other parts of Europe, poets in each area adapted the ideas to their local **vernacular** and musical styles. At the same time, professional musicians were developing new kinds of music. Composers added harmonies and began to use several melody lines together. Many lords had resident musicians. Harpists were usually the preferred soloists. Manorial musical groups often included musicians who played drums, portable organs, and different string and wind instruments.

the Vernacular

Throughout Europe, educated people wrote serious books in Latin. The Mass and Church music were written in Latin. Ordinary people spoke different regional languages. The local language of a region is called the vernacular. France had two vernaculars—*langue d'oc* in the south and *langue d'oeil* in the north. The original troubadours wrote in *langue d'oc*.

Traveling entertainers regularly toured through a region, stopping at manors, abbeys, and towns. The performers generally combined juggling, acrobatics, jokes, and music in their shows. They also recited chansons de geste—long poems

Rutebeuf

Rutebeuf was a traveling performer of the thirteenth century. He is thought to be the first entertainer to express popular opinions in the vernacular in France. He wrote funny and sarcastic poems about marriage, poverty, and similar everyday subjects. He made fun of merchants and other groups. His favorite targets were friars who traveled around Europe preaching. Rutebeuf also wrote some serious poems and plays.

◀ Musicians are shown playing for the Holy Roman Emperor in this fourteenth-century illustration. Their instruments include woodwinds, bowed strings, and a bagpipe (*right*).

describing the legendary feats of the Emperor Charlemagne and his knights—and other epic poems. Chansons de geste were very popular with knights. By the twelfth century, some lords began to hire performers for their households. **Minstrels**, as the performers came to be called, typically performed in the lord's hall during the midday dinner.

Indoor Entertainment and Games

People of all classes enjoyed many of the same games. Lords and peasants played chess, checkers, backgammon, and dice. They made bets on all sorts of games. They amused themselves by telling stories and riddles and singing songs. Outdoor games, such as blind man's bluff and lawn bowling, were popular with everyone.

Some activities were usually practiced only by people of one class. For instance, only wealthy women could do embroidery. The silk threads and fine fabrics needed for this pastime were very expensive. Playing cards were introduced toward the end of the Middle Ages, and for some time, they were available only to the upper class. Peasant men enjoyed watching cockfighting (battles between trained roosters) and bull baiting (battles between dogs and bulls).

Hunting

Hunting was extremely popular. Lords reserved for themselves the right to hunt deer and wild boars on their lands to put extra meat on the table. Peasants hunted hares and other small animals. Knights hunted on horseback with hunting dogs. In their households, they often had professional hunters, who tracked the prey and handled the dogs.

Hawking or falconry was hunting with birds of prey. This type of hunting was popular with noblewomen as well as men of all classes.

◀ Large stags, hunted in summer, were the favorite prey of nobles. The hunters used different types of dogs: bloodhounds to track the prey and hounds to drive the prey toward the hunters on horseback. After a deer was killed, everyone—including the dogs—got a share of the meat.

Hunting birds needed constant training and attention, and some knights kept their favorite falcons with them all the time, either on their wrists or a perch. Sometimes they hired falconers to train their birds.

Tournaments and Festivals

Tournaments began in the eleventh century. At first they were military exercises designed to help knights practice their skills during peacetime, but over the centuries, they developed into social occasions. As the philosophy of courtly love became popular and knights became interested in gaining the favor of ladies, women began attending tournaments. By the fifteenth century, tournaments lasted for several days and were accompanied by banquets and dancing.

Knights and ladies celebrated holidays in their manor houses, often in the company of vassals and friends. For villagers, some holidays were for family only, but others gave the community a chance to celebrate on the village green. Holidays were occasions on which to pray, play games, and eat heartily. Most holidays were determined by the Church calendar.

With the exception of Lent and the fall harvest season, every month had a holiday to break up the heavy work routine. On May Day (May 1),

◀ So many knights were injured in early tournaments that, over time, changes were made to reduce the violence. Knights began to use blunted instruments. Jousts, or combat between only two knights, were introduced in the twelfth century.

Social Dancing

Dancing was very popular. Peasant dancers sang and performed dance steps while holding hands. Knights and ladies sang and danced in a circle with hands clasped or danced in pairs to instrumental music. Preachers frequently spoke out against dancing, saying it was the work of the devil, but most people did not listen.

▲ This fifteenth-century illustration shows French shepherds dancing on the village green.

young people looked for flowers in the woods to celebrate spring. Saint John's Day (June 24) and All Saints' Day (November 1) were celebrated with bonfires. Easter gave villagers a week off from working for the lord, and Christmas gave them two weeks off. The date of the parish saint's festival varied from place to place but was often observed with an all-night vigil in church the night before, followed by morning Mass and celebrations. Guilds held processions and feasts on the day of their patron saint. Some guilds put on plays. The members of one English guild dressed up as Robin Hood and Little John and had an archery contest.

Competitions were a frequent part of festivals. Men took part in contests of strength, lifting sacks of grain or stones. Teams competed in rowdy ball games in which players hit, kicked, or carried a large ball toward a goal. Games often pitted two villages against each other or bachelors against married men. Women also competed in running races and ball games.

Villagers sometimes hired minstrels to perform for them. For many, the fun was just getting together with friends to sing, drink, and laugh for a while.

Moments of rest were often spent with friends and neighbors. Knights lounged after dark with their fellows. Ladies sat together, sewing or playing board games. Peasant women had a chance to talk together when they went to get water at the well. Plowmen stopped at alehouses to socialize with neighbors at the end of the day.

Natural and human events gradually brought about changes in medieval society. Wars caused some families to lose and others to gain lands and disrupted the lives of many others. Floods led to famines. The Black Death—a fourteenth-century epidemic of plague—changed the makeup of local populations in a few years. Technological advances, such as the spinning wheel, changed the way people worked. Peasants at times rebelled, even though their rebellions were always put down. Serfs slowly rid themselves of the taxes and fees they had once owed their lords. Many customs guiding family life and relations between classes persisted. As the Crusades ended and the Age of Exploration began in the fifteenth century, however, the age of feudalism and manorialism started to fade away.

c. 700
Manorialism is firmly established as peasants seek nobles' protection from invasions and wars.

c. 800-1300
Climate change occurs in Europe; the weather becomes warmer.

c. 900
Feudal relationships are firmly established between lords and vassals in many regions.

The widespread use of the wheeled plow, with an iron plate that digs into the soil, makes farm work easier.

c. 1000
The spice trade flourishes.

c. 1050
Knights begin to hold tournaments as practice for war.

1054
Christianity splits into two groups: the Roman Catholic Church with the pope based in Rome and the Eastern Orthodox Church with the patriarch based in Constantinople (now Istanbul).

1095-1099
Knights have the opportunity to practice chivalry in the First Crusade.

c. 1100
Philosophy of courtly love develops in southern France; troubadours write songs and poems about courtly love in the vernacular.

The fireplace is developed.

The first *chanson de geste* is written; it glorifies the military achievements of Charlemagne's knights.

c. 1100
Runaway serfs begin to be given freedom after living one year and one day in a town.

c. 1130
The woolen cloth industry is firmly established, leading to the introduction of technologies, such as the spinning wheel.

1152
Eleanor of Aquitaine marries Henry of Anjou, the future king of England. She surrounds herself with poets and musicians, who help her spread the ideas of courtly love throughout much of Europe.

c. 1160
Poets and ideas about courtly love flourish at the court of Marie, countess of Champagne.

c. 1170
William Marshal goes into the service of King Henry II of England.

c. 1200
Musicians begin writing music with two or more melody lines, with nonreligious subject matter, and words in the vernacular.

The open-field system of agriculture is widespread.

Fulling mills begin to be built.

c. 1230
Sumptuary laws begin to be issued. Edward II of England enforces sumptuary laws in the early fourteenth century.

1245-1280
Rutebeuf writes his popular works.

1265
Representatives of towns and countryside are called to English Parliament for the first time.

c. 1300-1500
European cities start to make rules for a cleaner environment.

1314-1316
Extremely bad weather leads to poor crops and famine.

1328
French royal family takes control of most of land today known as France.

1347-1351
The Black Death strikes Europe, killing about forty million people.

1381
Peasants revolt in England.

c. 1400
Tournaments become social occasions.

Minstrels from different parts of Europe exchange ideas at "minstrel schools," held during Lent when performances are not allowed.

1450
The printing press is developed.

1492
Christians defeat Muslims in Spain, ending the last chivalric war for religion.

Source References:

[1] **C. Warren Hollister.** *Medieval Europe: A Short History*, Wiley, 1964, p. 1.

[2] **Oath of fealty, 1127. Quoted in T. F. X. Noble et al.,** *Western Civilization: The Continuing Experiment*, **Vol. 1, Houghton Mifflin, 1998, p. 313.**

[3] **Friar Berthold von Regensburg. Quoted in P. Speed,** *Those Who Worked: An Anthology of Medieval Sources*, **Italica Press, 1997, p. 34.**

[4] *Seneschaucie*, **treatise on estate management. Quoted in F. and J. Gies,** *Life in a Medieval Village*, **Harper Perennial, 1990, p. 50.**

[5] *Fleta*, **treatise on law and administration. Quoted in P. Speed, see** *above*, **p. 38.**

[6] **Montepescali, Italy, 1427. Quoted in P. Speed, see** *above*, **p. 31.**

[7] **Wimeswould, England, 1425. Quoted in P. Speed, see** *above*, **p. 32.**

[8] **Addington Manor Rolls, England, 1433. Quoted in P. Speed, see** *above*, **p. 33.**

[9] **Bartholomaeus Anglicus, monk. Quoted in F. and J. Gies,** *Marriage and the Family in the Middle Ages*, **Harper & Row, 1987, p. 196.**

[10] **G. de Lorris and J. de Meun.** *The Romance of the Rose*, **Harry W. Robbins, trans., E. P. Dutton, 1962, p. 45.**

[11] **Will of Stephen Thomas, 1417–1418. Quoted in E. Power,** *Medieval Women*, **Cambridge University Press, 1975, p. 43.**

[12] **Anthony Fitzherbert,** *Boke of Husbandrie*. **Quoted in P. Speed, see** *above*, **p. 162.**

[13] **"Sir Gawain and the Green Knight" in M. H. Abrams et al.,** *The Norton Anthology of English Literature*, **Vol. 1, revised. W. W. Norton, 1968, p. 238. Quoted in M. Wade Labarge,** *Mistress, Maids, and Men: Baronial Life in the Thirteenth Century*, **Phoenix, 2003, p. 79.**

[14] **English schoolboy. Quoted in M. Wade Labarge, see** *above*, **p. 79.**

[15] **William Langland,** *Piers the Ploughman*. **Quoted in P. Speed, see** *above*, **p. 29.**

abbesses   Nuns who head up a monastery of nuns

arable   Good for plowing and growing crops

arson   A fire that is purposely set

barbarian   An ancient Greek word used by Romans and later Europeans to describe foreigners. It suggests that foreigners are wild, brutal, and savage.

caravans   Travelers who group together to help each other, usually in a hostile region, such as a desert

close   A family's homestead, including the house, outbuildings, and vegetable garden

cottars   Poor villagers who lived in small cottages

Crusades   Wars fought between Christians and Muslims, heretics, and pagans

demesne   Arable land reserved for the lord and cultivated for him

dowry/dowries   The money, goods, land, and possessions that a woman brings to her husband in marriage

draft animals   A team of animals, such as oxen, mules, or horses, used to pull a cart or wagon

estate   All the manors belonging to one lord

estate steward   The chief administrator of a lord's manors

fealty   Loyalty a vassal owed to his lord

feudalism   A term historians use for the system that guided relationships between knights and their lords

fief   Land or other payment a knight received from a lord

foraging   Looking for food or raw materials

freemen   Peasants who rented land from a lord but were not obligated to provide other services

fuller   Person who shrinks and thickens wool cloth before it is dyed and used to make clothing

garrison   A group of knights stationed in a lord's manor to defend it

harrow   To break up large clods of soil left after plowing a field

homage   A vassal's pledge to serve his lord

manor   Property held by a lord that included his house, peasant village, and lands

manorialism   A term historians use for the system governing relations between a lord and his serfs

Mass   The religious rite that includes the ritual eating of bread and drinking of wine, which is part of Catholic services; the two substances symbolize the body and blood of Jesus. The ritual recalls the last meal he shared with his apostles.

medieval   A word that relates to and describes the Middle Ages

minstrels   Performers who combined different types of entertainment, such as acrobatics, juggling, telling jokes, playing music, and reciting poetry

moat   A wide ditch surrounding a manor or castle

parapets   High walls surrounding the lord's close, designed to protect it from enemy attack

parliaments   Conferences to discuss public affairs, or the organization of political groups to form a government

rank   A person's position in society

resin   A liquid substance that drips out of many trees, such as amber and pine rosin; resins were used as fuel for lamps in the Middle Ages.

Roman Empire   The people and lands that belonged to ancient Rome, consisting of most of southern Europe and northern Africa from Britain to the Middle East

romances   Popular stories and poems about knightly adventures and courtly love

serf   A peasant who did work for a lord in exchange for protection and land; in the Middle Ages, serfs could not move from the manor without the lord's permission.

tallage   A tax a lord could require his serfs to pay at any time without giving a reason

threshing   Separating the kernels of grain from the husks by beating them with a stick

tournaments   Mock battle in which knights practiced their military skills

trestle tables   Tables that are assembled from separate sets of legs and large pieces of wood for the top

troubadours   Poets who sang about courtly love

vassal   A knight who swears to serve another knight

vernacular   The dialect or language of a region

waste   An uncultivated area where villagers gathered wild plants, nuts, and berries

wet nurses   Women who replaced mothers in caring for children, usually starting with suckling the child

winnowing   Blowing away the husks from the kernels of grain

woodland   A forested, marshy, or high area with good pasture, suitable for raising sheep or cattle

furtheR InformatioN

Books:

Barter, James. *Life in a Medieval Village.* Farmington Hills, MI: Lucent Books, 2003.

Dawson, Imogen. *Clothes and Crafts in the Middle Ages.* Milwaukee, WI: Gareth Stevens, 2000.

Eastwood, Kay. *Medieval Society.* New York: Crabtree Publishers, 2004.

Eastwood, Kay. *Women and Girls in the Middle Ages.* New York: Crabtree Publishers, 2004.

Hinds, Kathryn. *The Countryside.* New York: Benchmark Books, 2001.

Hinds, Kathryn. *Medieval England.* New York: Marshall Cavendish, 2001.

Web Sites:

The following web sites provide information and links to other sites:

Berkeley Digital Library SunSITE
sunsite.berkeley.edu
Click on "Catalogs and Indexes," "KidsClick!," and then "Geography/History/Biography: World History."
Then click on "Middle Ages" for links to many useful sites on life, art, and events of the Middle Ages.

Exhibits Collection: The Middle Ages
www.learner.org/exhibits/middleages
This site covers many topics about everyday life during medieval times, including feudalism, homes, and the arts.

Librarians' Index to the Internet
lii.org
Under "History," click on "Middle Ages" for links to sites about medieval life, culture, and politics.

Medieval Technology Pages
scholar.chem.nyu.edu/tekpages/Subjects.html
This site has articles explaining medieval technology—from horse harnesses to plows to soap.

NetSERF: The Internet Connection for Medieval Resources
www.netserf.org
Look under "Culture" and "Music" for various links. Explore "Feudalism" and "Social History" under the "History" heading.

Videos/DVDs:

Just the Facts: The Middle Ages. Goldhil Home Media, 2001. (VHS)

Life in the Middle Ages: Social Structure in the Middle Ages (vol. 8). Schlessinger Media, 2002. (VHS)